# The 3 Dots

Antony Melvin D Paul

BookLeaf Publishing

India | USA | UK

Presentation by *BookLeaf Publishing*

Web: www.bookleafpub.com

E-mail: info@bookleafpub.com

ISBN: 9789363317642

First edition 2024

# ACKNOWLEDGEMENT

First and foremost, I extend my deepest gratitude to the Almighty for bestowing upon me the talent and skills that have shaped my journey. Your divine guidance has been my constant companion.

To my mother, my most inspiring friend, your unwavering support and boundless love have been my greatest source of strength. You have always believed in me, and for that, I am eternally grateful.

To my loving wife and champion son, your pride in me fuels my determination. Your love and encouragement have been my pillars of support, and I am blessed to have you by my side.

To my father, who has trained me to be the best in all that I do, your wisdom and guidance have been invaluable. You have instilled in me the values of hard work and perseverance, and for that, I am forever thankful.

To my lovely younger twin sisters, your unwavering faith and love have been a constant source of joy and motivation. Your belief in me has kept me going, even in the toughest times.

To those very few who are always embedded in my heart, your presence in my life has been a blessing. Your support and love have been my anchor.

And to my special friend, Shree, thank you for sharing this opportunity and for keeping the writer in me alive. Your encouragement and belief in my abilities have been instrumental in this journey.

With heartfelt gratitude,

Antony Melvin D Paul

# PREFACE

In a world brimming with diverse experiences and endless opportunities for growth, I have been fortunate to traverse a path that intertwines training, academia, culinary arts, sports, and writing. This book is a culmination of my journey, a tapestry woven with threads of knowledge, passion, and creativity.

My foray into training has allowed me to witness the transformative power of education and skill development. Through tailored programs, I have had the privilege of guiding individuals toward their goals, fostering a culture of continuous improvement and empowerment.

Academia has been a cornerstone of my life, driving me to delve deep into the realms of knowledge and contribute to scholarly discourse. The pursuit of learning has not only enriched my understanding but also fueled my desire to share insights with others.

Cooking, a delightful art form, has been a source of joy and experimentation. The kitchen is my canvas, where flavors and techniques come together to create culinary masterpieces. This passion for cooking is paralleled by my enthusiasm for sports, where I find both solace and exhilaration. Engaging in sports has taught me the value of perseverance, teamwork, and the sheer joy of physical activity.

Writing, however, is where all these experiences converge. It is through the written word that I can share my journey, inspire others, and offer a unique perspective on the world. This book is a reflection of my multifaceted life, an invitation to explore the intersections of training, academia, cooking, sports, and writing.

I hope that as you turn these pages, you find inspiration, insight, and a renewed appreciation for the myriad ways in which our passions shape our lives.

Warm regards,

Antony Melvin D Paul

# My Little White Paper

In the quiet corners of existence,
Lies my little white paper,
A canvas unmarked, pristine,
Waiting for life's ink to shape it.

Life, they say, is as simple as paper,
A blank slate upon which we write,
With words that dance like fireflies,
Or stumble like awkward first steps.

I cradle my paper, delicate and thin,
Its edges whispering secrets of eternity,
And I wonder: what shall I inscribe?
A comedy? A tragedy? A love story?

Perhaps I'll sketch laughter in bold strokes,
Splattering ink like raindrops on glass,
Drawing smiles that stretch across the page,
And giggles that echo through time.

Or maybe I'll weave melancholy threads,
Ink bleeding like tears from a wounded heart,
Creating shadows that linger in the margins,
Aching with the weight of unspoken dreams.

But wait! Life isn't just black and white,
It's the grey of uncertainty, the hues of hope,
The vibrant colors of sunrise after storm,
And the soft pastels of whispered promises.

So, my little white paper, let's write:
Let's scribble joy in sunflower yellow,
Trace courage in indigo waves,
And fold origami cranes of resilience.

Let's ink love letters to the moon,
And draw constellations of possibility,
For life is more than mere survival,
It's the art of turning paper into poetry.

And when the inkwell runs dry,
When my fingers ache from endless creation,
I'll fold my paper into a paper boat,
And set it adrift on the river of time.

May it sail toward sunsets and rainbows,
Carrying laughter, tears, and whispered wishes,
A testament to the magic of ordinary moments,
And the extraordinary stories we write.

My little white paper, you're not empty,
You're a universe waiting to be explored,
A canvas for dreams, a vessel for hope,
And in your simplicity, lies boundless beauty.

# Chalk and the Blackboard

In a world of screens and digital streams,
Where technology reigns and innovation gleams,
Let us not forget the simple things,
The chalk and blackboard, where learning
springs.

With a piece of chalk, so humble and small,
We draw out dreams, we answer the call.
On the blackboard's slate, ideas take flight,
In elegant strokes, we shed new light.

Amidst the surge of modern might,
Old-school tools still shine so bright.
Elegant, powerful, efficient, and true,
They teach us lessons, both old and new.

In simplicity, there's a timeless grace,
A quiet strength, a steady pace.
Forgotten now, but still so grand,
The chalk and blackboard take a stand.

They whisper softly, "Remember me,
In my simplicity, there's power to see.
Great heights are reached with humble starts,
With chalk in hand and open hearts."

So let us rekindle the old-school flame,
In the dance of chalk, we'll find our name.
For in the simplest things, we often find,
The most profound truths, the clearest mind.

# The Grumble Parade

In a town not far but not too near,
Lived folks who grumbled year after year.
With blessings plenty,and fortunes grand,
Yet they compared and couldn't understand.

"Oh, look at Jane, her house so tall,
Why isn't mine the best of all?"
"Tom's got a car that's shiny and new,
Why can't I have a better one too?"

They'd gather each day,in the Grumble Parade,
With egos inflated, complaints displayed.
"My coffee's too cold, my soup's too hot,
My neighbor's got things that I have not!"

They'd whine and moan and sigh and groan,
Ignoring the blessings they already owned.
A roof overhead, and food on their plate,
But gratitude? Oh, that could wait.

One day a wise man, with a twinkle in his eye,
Said,
"Why not give gratitude a try? Count your
blessings,
big and small, and you'll see, you have it all."

But the folks just scoffed and rolled their eyes,
"Gratitude? Oh, what a surprise!
We'd rather compare, and moan and groan,
It's much more fun than being alone."

They marched on, in their Grumble Parade,
With egos intact and complaints displayed.
But deep down inside, they knew it was true,
Gratitude could change their view.

So next time you find yourself in a grumble,
Remember this tale and try to be humble.
Count your blessings, and you'll soon see,
Life's pretty great; just let it be!

# Love Found, Love Lost, Love everlasting

From the moment of birth, a love so pure,
A mother's embrace, a bond that's sure.
Unconditional, steadfast, and true,
A guiding light in all we do.

Her love shapes our lives, like clay in her hands,
Inspires our dreams and helps us to stand.
She teaches with patience, wisdom, and grace,
Her love is a haven, a warm, safe place.

But when it's lost, a void so deep,
A heart that aches, a soul that weeps.
The world feels colder, shadows grow long,
Yet her love's imprint remains strong.

Love comes in many forms, we find,
In friends, in family, in hearts so kind.
It teaches us lessons, both gentle and tough,
That love is eternal and always enough.

To understand love, we must open our hearts,
Embrace its beauty in all its parts.
For love is the thread that weaves through our
days,
A tapestry of life, in countless ways.

A mother's love, the first we know,
Sets the stage for love to grow.
In every hug, in every tear,
Her love remains forever near.

# Brave Minds

As the dark clouds swelled vigorously,
Threatening to rain down plagues of diseases,
Holding to ransom, the entire humanity,
Challenging the mere mortals to defend, survive,
and thrive.

When all looked gloomy, all looked gone,
A few knights dared to mount horses.These
knights rode against the odds,
They rode with purpose; they rode with focus.

For they donned not just the mantle to save the
earth,
But they were a few good women and men with
'Brave Minds'
With zeal in their stride and the passion to cure,
They challenged the conventional and rode to
make an impact.

For they knew nothing can stop a brave mind,
nothing can slow them down,
They rode with purpose, they rode with focus.

Touching lives on their way, changing the weak
into strong,
Gathering in their stride, many more who joined,
A few now become many, and the many,
becoming many more.

For they knew nothing can stop a brave mind,
nothing can slow them down.
The dark clouds took notice, for there was an
uprising,
Lay from below, the voices bellowed – bring it
on, for we are the brave minds,
We march with purpose; we march with focus.

Nothing will dare slow them down, nor can it
tire them,
For they are the brave minds, standing between
the plague and the meek,
For until they live, there will always be life and
celebration of live."

# A dream

In the quiet of the night, when stars gleam
bright,
A dream takes flight, soaring to a wondrous
height.
With a heart full of hope and a mind set to
scheme,
Remember, my friend, it all starts with a dream.

But dreaming alone won't make it come true,
You need a plan, a goal, and a to-do.
Wake up each morning with a fire in your soul,
Take that first step, and you're on a roll.

With grit and grind, and a sprinkle of fun,
You'll find that the journey has just begun.
There'll be bumps and bruises, and maybe a fall,
But get up, dust off, and stand tall.

For every setback is a setup for a comeback,
Keep pushing forward, never look back.
Laugh at the hurdles, smile at the pain,
For every drop of sweat is another gain.

Believe in yourself and the power within,
With hard work and patience, you'll surely win.
Dream big, work hard, and never say never,
For dreams do come true if you endeavor.

And when you reach the top, with a view so
grand,
You'll laugh and say, "I knew I could, I
planned!"
Here's to dreams and making them real,
With a dash of humorand a heart full of zeal.

# Friends are pearls

In the oyster of life, woven with care,
There are threads of pearl, friendships rare.
When the world feels heavy and skies turn gray,
A friend steps in, lighting the way.

With laughter and tears, they stand by your side,
In moments of joy and times you've cried.
Their presence, a balm, a comforting touch,
In the chaos of life, they mean so much.

Friends are the pillars that hold us upright,
Guiding us through the darkest night.
With words of wisdom and hearts so true,
They lift us up when we're feeling blue.

In the dance of life, they lead with grace,
A smile, a hug, a warm embrace.
They see our dreams and cheer us on,
Believing in us, from dusk till dawn.

Through thick and thin, they never sway,
Their love, a beacon, come what may.
In the silence of doubt, their voices ring,
Encouraging us to spread our wings.

For friends are the treasures, priceless and rare,
A gift from the heavens, beyond compare.
They shape our lives with gentle hands,
Helping us grow and understand.

Cherish your friends, hold them near,
For they are the ones who banish fear.
In the book of life, they write a line,
A story of love, forever divine.

# The Unexplained Bond

In the heart of a home, where love resides,
A father and child, side by side.
With gentle hands and a guiding light,
A father's love, pure and bright.

From the first steps to the dreams that soar,
He stands as a friend, and so much more.
With wisdom shared and stories told,
He gives his child the courage to be bold.

"Fly high," he says, "The world is yours,
With open skies and endless shores."
He nurtures dreams with tender care,
A bond so strong, beyond compare.

As years go by and seasons change,
Their relationship blossoms, never strange.
From playful days to heartfelt talks,
Together they walk on life's winding walks.

A father's love, a steady hand,
Helping his child to understand.
That in this world, with all its strife,
He'll always be there, a friend for life.

And as the child grows, with wings to fly,
They look back with love and never sigh.
For in their hearts, they hold a place,
For the man who gave them strength and grace.

In time, the roles may gently shift,
The child now gives a precious gift.
With love and care, they stand by his side,
A bond unbroken, a source of pride.

For fathers and children, a circle complete,
With love and friendship, life is sweet.
Together they face, whatever may come,
A father and child, forever one.

# The firefly

In the stillness of a night, when shadows creep,
A tiny firefly begins to leap.
With a flicker of light, so small yet bright,
It dances through the velvet night.

Life, like a firefly, glows in the dark,
A beacon of hope, a tiny spark.
Even when the world seems cold and gray,
Its light whispers, "There is a way."

Through trials and tribulations, we may roam,
But within us all, there's a light to guide us
home.
In the darkest hours, when hope seems lost,
Remember the firefly, no matter the cost.

It flutters on, with courage and grace,
Lighting up the night, finding its place.
So too must we, with hearts full of fire,
Believe in ourselves, and never tire.

For every night gives way to dawn,
And every struggle makes us strong.
With faith and hope, we tread the path,
Knowing that light will follow the aftermath.

So let the firefly be your guide,
A symbol of hope, by your side.
In the darkest of nights, let your spirit fly,
For there's always light on the other side.

# Woman the Mitochondria

In the tale of life, she threads her gold,
A story of strength forever told.
Her laughter, a symphony, bright and clear,
Her wisdom, a compass, always near.

She nurtures dreams with tender care,
A guardian of hope, always there.
Her hands, a cradle, her heart, a guide,
In her embrace, we find our stride.

Through storms and sunshine, she remains,
A beacon of light, through joys and pains.
Her influence, a garden, lush and green,
In her presence, we feel serene.

Honor her journey, cherish her soul,
For in her essence, we become whole.
A force of nature, gentle and grand,
In her, the future of humankind stands.

# Raise above the storms

In the vast expanse of life's great sea,
Where waves of challenge rise,
We steer our ship through stormy gales,
Beneath uncertain skies.

With courage as our guiding star,
And hope our steadfast sail,
We face the tempests of our days,
And through the storms prevail.

For every wave that crashes down,
And every gust that roars,
We find our strength within ourselves,
In tales of days before.

Our stories are the anchors,
That keep us safe and sound,
In the darkest nights and fiercest storms,
It's where our hope is found.

So let us sail with hearts of steel,
And spirits brave and free,
For in the trials we endure,
Our true selves we shall see.

# Life is a classroom

In the quiet of the classroom,
Where wisdom softly speaks,
A teacher's voice, a guiding light,
In every heart, it seeks.

With patience and with kindness,
They nurture dreams and hopes,
In every lesson, every word,
They hand us life's great ropes.

They come in many forms and ways,
A mentor, friend, or guide,
In every challenge, every praise,
They walk right by our side.

Through books and tales, through trials and
tests,
They shape the minds they mold,
In every heart, a lasting mark,
Their stories gently told.

To the ones who light our paths,
And help us find our way,
We owe a debt of gratitude,
In every single day.

For in their hands, the future lies,
In every child they see,
A world of endless possibilities,
A better place to be.

So here's to teachers, near and far,
In classrooms, homes, and more,
For all the ways they touch our lives,
We thank them evermore.

# Twins the double blessing

In the fabric of life, so bright,
With threads of love and care,
There shines a bond, so pure and true,
A sister's love to share.

With laughter that can light the dark,
And smiles that chase away,
The shadows of our deepest fears,
And brighten every day.

Through childhood dreams and secret schemes,
And whispers in the night,
A sister's heart is always there,
A beacon of pure light.

In moments of both joy and pain,
Her presence is a balm,
A steady hand, a listening ear,
A voice that brings us calm.

For in her eyes, we see our past,
And futures yet to be,
A sister's love, a precious gift,
From now till eternity.

So here's to sisters, near and far,
In every form, they come,
For all the ways they touch our lives,
And make our hearts feel home.

# I don't walk alone

In the yards of our shared life,
You are the thread of gold,
A lover, wife, and dearest friend,
With a heart so brave and bold.

Your trust, a beacon in the night,
Guides me through the storm,
In your embrace, I find my strength,
In your love, I am reborn.

Your support, a steadfast pillar,
In times both good and bad,
With you, I face the world unafraid,
In joy and when I'm afraid.

Your caring touch, a gentle whisper of 'I love you',
That soothes my weary soul,
In your arms, I find my peace,
In your love, I am whole.

With you, I feel secure and proud,
In every step we take,
Together, we build dreams anew,
With every dawn, we wake.

So here's to you, my cherished one,
My partner, love, and guide,
In you, I've found my everything,
Forever by my side.

# No room for Negativity

In the garden of our minds,
Where thoughts and dreams do grow,
We must tend with care and love,
And let the good seeds sow.

Steer clear of shadows, dark and cold,
Where negativity lies,
For in the light of hope and joy,
Our spirits truly rise.

Avoid the ones who bring you down,
With words that sting and bite,
Surround yourself with those who lift,
And fill your heart with light.

For in the company of love,
And friends who truly care,
We find the strength to stand our ground,
And face what life may bear.

Let not the harsh words of the world,
Define your worth or way,
For you are strong, and you are bright,
A beacon in the fray.

So guard your heart and guard your mind,
From negativity's snare,
And let your soul be filled with light,
With love beyond compare.

# Tears in the rain

In the quiet of the storm, they stand tall,
Dousing tears in the rain, they never fall.
Though their hearts ache with silent cries,
They wear a smile, hiding the pain in their eyes.

Brave faces in the midst of sorrow,
They fight through the night, hoping for
tomorrow.
Their strength is a beacon, a silent plea,
For someone to notice, for someone to see.

It's touching—this courage, this silent fight,
A testament to their unyielding might.
But let us not be blind to their hidden pain,
For even the strongest need shelter from the rain.

So, let us be the comfort, the gentle hand,
To lift them up, to help them stand.
For in their strength, they show us the way,
To be kind, to be there every single day.

# Keep the child alive

As the years go by and hair turns grey,
Let's keep the child in us at play.
For life is brighter, full of cheer,
When we embrace our inner dear.

Jump in puddles, dance in the rain,
Laugh out loud, forget the pain.
Wear silly hats, make funny faces,
Find joy in the simplest places.

Build sandcastles, fly a kite,
Stay up late, watch stars at night.
Tell tall tales, play hide and seek,
Let your spirit be wild and unique.

For growing old is just a guise,
The real fun's in our youthful eyes.
So, let's be playful, let's be free,
And life will be as sweet as can be.

# Failure teaches

Do not fear the stumble, the fall,
For in failure, we learn to stand tall.
Each misstep, a lesson in disguise,
A chance to grow, to become wise.

Embrace the fall, the bruises, the scars,
They shape who we are like the night shapes the stars.
In every setback, there's a hidden gain,
A strength, a wisdom, born from the pain.

Failure is not the end, but a start,
A journey to mend, to strengthen the heart.
It teaches us courage, to rise once more,
To face the world, to open new doors.

So, welcome the failures, the trials, the strife,
They are the teachers in the school of life.
For in each fall, we find our way,
To a brighter, stronger, better day.

Each failure is a seed, planted deep,
In the soil of our soul, where dreams sleep.
With time and care, it starts to grow,
Into strength and wisdom, that we show.

# Prayer a bridge

In the stillness of the night, we find,
A moment to quiet the restless mind.
Whispers to the universe, soft and clear,
A prayer, a hope, a wish sincere.

No need for words of ancient lore,
Just a heart that seeks to explore.
A connection deep, a silent plea,
To the vast unknown, to the cosmic sea.

Prayer is the bridge to our inner light,
A way to find peace in the darkest night.
It fills our soul, renews our fire,
A source of strength, a well of desire.

In moments of doubt, in times of strife,
Prayer is the compass, the guide in life.
It grounds us, lifts us, helps us see,
The beauty in all, the possibility.

So, let us pray, in our own way,
To connect, to heal, to find our sway.
For in these whispers, we discover anew,
The power within, the strength to pursue.

# The sharpener

In a world of endless noise and haste,
Be the sharpener, with gentle grace.
Not just a voice that echoes loud,
But a guide who stands out in the crowd.

Like a blade that hones the edge, sharpens skills,
fulfills the pledge.
To touch each life that comes your way,
And brighten up their darkest day.
Empower others, let them see,

The strength within, their destiny.
With every word and every deed,
Plant the seeds that they might need.

Leave a mark, indelible and true,
In hearts and minds, in all they do.
For in the end, it's not the fame,
But lives improved that built your name.

Be the sharpener, kind and wise,
Lift others up, help them rise.
For in this journey, side by side,
We find our purpose and our pride.

# Life is to be celebrated

In the morning's gentle glow,
Where the sun begins to rise,
We find the joy in simple things,
In laughter, love, and skies.

Each moment is a treasure,
A gift we hold so dear,
In the dance of daily wonders,
Life's beauty is so clear.

Celebrate the little things,
A smile, a touch, a song,
For in these fleeting moments,
Our hearts are made strong.

Embrace the highs and lows,
The journey's winding way,
For every step we take in life,
Brings light into our day.

So let us raise our voices,
In gratitude and cheer,
For life is truly precious,
A gift we hold so near.

# Expectations–a ditcher

In the quiet of the night, when dreams take
flight,
We search for solace, for a guiding light.
Yet in the shadows, where doubts reside,
We find the strength we hold inside.

Expectations from others, a fragile thread,
Can break and leave us filled with dread.
But within our hearts, a fire burns bright,
A beacon of hope in the darkest night.

Trust not in promises nor in fleeting praise,
For they may falter in life's maze.
Instead, look inward, where courage lies,
In the depths of your soul, let it rise.

For you are the master of your fate,
The architect of your own state.
Believe in yourself with unwavering might,
And you'll conquer the challenges in sight.

So let go of the need for others' grace,
Embrace your journey, set your pace.
For in self-belief, you'll find the key,
To unlock your potential, to truly be free.

# Smile–the best attire to wear

In the tapestry of life, woven with care,
A smile is the finest attire one can wear.
It brightens the day, like the morning sun,
A silent promise that joy has begun.

Behind every smile, a story untold,
Of battles fought, and hearts consoled.
Yet through the grief, the pain, the strife,
A smile emerges, a beacon of life.

It whispers softly, "All will be well,"
A gentle reminder, a comforting spell.
For in the curve of lips, hope resides,
A testament to strength that never hides.

No matter the sorrow, the tears that fall,
A smile can conquer, can stand tall.
It bridges the gap between hearts and souls,
A universal language that makes us whole.

Wear your smile with grace and pride,
Let it be your armor, your guide.
For in its warmth, the world will see,
The beauty of resilience, the power of "me."

# Lost but not forgotten

In the garden of memories, where time stands
still,
A loved one's presence lingers, a void to fill.
Though they may be lost, their essence remains,
In whispers of the wind, in gentle rains.

Their laughter echoes in the silent night,
A beacon of love, a guiding light.
Though distance and time may keep us apart,
They live forever in the depths of our hearts.

True love is patient; it knows no bounds,
It waits in silence, where hope resounds.
For love that is true, never fades away,
It endures the night and welcomes the day.

In the tapestry of life, woven with care,
Their spirit is a thread, always there.
Though we may search and wander far,
True love waits, like a steadfast star.

Hold on to the memories, cherish the past,
For love that is true will always last.
And in the journey, when the time is right,
True love will find you, like morning light.

# Brothers by Heart

From different mothers, different homes,
Yet in this family, together we roam.

Bound not by blood, but by love so true,
Brothers-in-law, a bond we grew.

You took my hand, welcomed me in,
With open hearts, our journey did begin.

In laughter and tears, through thick and thin,
Unconditional love, where do I begin?

You stand by my side, a pillar so strong,
In this new family, where we belong.

With every smile, every shared glance,
You give me courage, a second chance.

Through life's ups and downs, we never part,
For brothers-in-law, are brothers by heart.

In this family, we've found our place,
Together we thrive, with love and grace.

# Three Dots of Love

In the sacred dance of life, three dots align,
A trinity of love, divine and kind.
Father, Son, and Spirit, a holy embrace,
In their unity, we find our place.

A hug, a gesture pure and true,
Arms wrapped tight, hearts renew.
In person, warmth and solace flow,
A silent promise, love's gentle glow.

Yet in this digital age, we see,
Three dots appear, a trinity.
An emoji hug, a symbol bright,
A touch of love in the virtual night.

But can pixels match the power felt,
When in real arms, our worries melt?
A hug in person, a sacred rite,
Transforms the dark into light.

Three dots, three forms, love's holy trine,
In every hug, a touch is divine.
Whether in flesh or on a screen,

A choice that one needs to teem.